THE HONOR CODE

A 21-DAY PATHWAY TO

"Maximizing Your Honor for Greatness"

BY

DONTRELL GREEN

Foreword by Steven Halliburton

To request permissions, contact the author at greendontrell41@yahoo.com

Published By Writing in Faith
IAmWritingInFaith.com

Cover Design By Cherese Agee
Reseagee.com

Dontrell Green (Text)

ISBN 13: 978-1-7353541-8-7

CONTENTS

DEDICATION

I dedicate this book to Angela Green, Glenda Green, and LaVerne DeBose my three mothers who have raised me and taught me everything about what it means to honor, trust God, and love others. You all have been my inspiration and I thank God every day for placing you in my life. Although you're not here physically, you will always remain in my heart, and I know from heaven you are smiling down upon me. The world needs more mothers like you and I honor you today and forever.

ACKNOWLEDGEMENTS

I would like to acknowledge my beautiful wife, Faith F. Green, whom I've now had the opportunity and privilege to be married to for 5 years. My love, you are my everything and without you, I wouldn't be the man I am today. You are my biggest fan, supporter and the motivation behind my writing as well as my success. I thank you and honor you for giving me the time and grace to write these last 7 months and for your continued prayers and love. Faith, I want you to know how much I love you and how grateful I am to have you in my life, with you, my dreams have come true. You are a perfect portrait ready to be discovered and I will always honor you no matter what life may bring.

I would like to also acknowledge all five of my precious children for giving me the space, time and respect to write something of this magnitude while away from them to focus on writing and getting this done in an appropriate manner of time. The joy and smiles on your faces make me strive and push even harder to be a better father and it challenges me to go beyond all limitations and all odds. I honor you all and honor God for entrusting and allowing me to be your father. Daddy loves you more than life itself. Always walk upright before the Lord and with great humility. I declare the favor of the Lord upon you in every aspect of your life and divine blessing. A'Lylah, Jace'yon, Dontrell Jr. Donzell, and Devine Green, I love you and may the honor of God's glory shine upon you.

To Agents of Change and Transformation Mentorship Family, I honor you and thank you for helping to mode me, praying for me, and believing in me. You all keep me focused more than you know and because of that, I am the prophet and prophetic voice I am today. I love all of you dearly and couldn't do it without you.

Also, unto my Ignite Nations Global family and friends, I thank you and appreciate you. When I wanted to give up and throw in the towel you were right there giving me the word of the Lord and telling me to keep going. Your commitment to see others grow and love them despite who they are is truly an inspiration and has impacted my life greatly. Thank you once more and don't stop being such an awesome family, you're doing a great work.

My brother and friend, Apostle Steven Halliburton, you are an incredible brilliant man of God and I'm honored to have you in my life and my corner. Over the last 2 years, I've watched as our friendship has grown abundantly in communication, love, and honor, and because of that, I'm a better person. Thank you for your loyalty, correction, listening ear and for being a part of this amazing project by giving your yes and dedication to write the foreword for this book. I will always be indebted and once more, I honor you, sir.

I also want to give thanks and recognition to my mother-in-law and Father-in-law, Adrian and Denise Fields. Since I've grown to know you both, it has been a tremendous blessing and I'm truly grateful that you all have accepted me as a son. As I've taken the opportunity to write this book, you have been there every step of the way to encourage me and support me and because of that, I will forever honor you. Thanks for your wisdom and love, you are the true MVP.

Finally, I would like to take the time to acknowledge my spiritual mother, Madeline James. I appreciate your wisdom, guidance, and leadership. Thank you for correcting, for challenging and stewarding me in the place of purity and love. There have been times I wanted to quit, but you never let me stop and because of that I'm grateful and I give you honor. You are the true definition of what spiritual parents are supposed to look like and I pray that one day there be more mothers to arise like you. I truly honor and admire you. Thank you for your discipleship.

AUTHOR ENDORSEMENTS

In the book, "Honor Code," Dontrell Green does a great job of reintroducing us to the subject of honor in the Body of Christ. Where honor has been misused, Dontrell shares with us how to walk in a lifestyle of honor properly and how a lifestyle of honor opens the blessings of God in our lives. As you read this book, you will get a greater revelation of how to apply honor daily in every area of your life, and it will shift your life.

Madeline James

Madeline James Ministries,

Author of Mastering Your Warfare

The Honor Code by Dontrell Green is an on-time, anointed, message for the merging together of generations in the Body of Christ.

It will be used to establish wisdom and strengthen the foundation of a generation rising to lead us into the great Harvest.

Monica Ramey

Founder of Monica Ramey Ministries,

Author of Walking In Dominion

It never ceases to amaze me how one prophetic word can shift the trajectory of someone's life and bring about the revelation of God's hidden treasures. This is exactly what happened to Dontrell Green when a pastor, spoke life-giving words to him about honor and the blessings of God. We are now beneficiaries of the magnificent revelations and wisdom imparted through this 21-day journey exploring the importance of honor in our lives. Let your life be transformed by the renewing of your mind by this Holy Spirit-inspired book, The Honor Code.

Dr. Shanicka N. Scarbrough
Author of Power to Heal Your Heart

In this book, you will find many ways in which honor can be shown towards each other in life, in family, in work relationships, and in our walk with God.

Prophet Dontrell looks at so many different aspects of honor throughout this 21-day journey. You will be encouraged and challenged to allow God to work in you and through you. Honor is something that cannot be forced but is something that flows out of a heart for God and from a heart towards others. This book will be a great blessing to you and will help you in many practical ways. Honor can be a very powerful force in your life. Let's all together endeavor to keep the Honor Code.

Bishop Greg D Gill
Ever-Increasing Ministries
Calgary, Alberta
Canada

In the book, Honor Code, Dontrell Green outlines the importance of honor to God as well as how it starts within the home. He indicates that this is something to be taught to be executed within one's life. Dontrell gives specific instructions on how to honor God for the simple things and how the manifestation will begin to form in one's life. As you meditate on this 21-day pathway, it will guide you step by step on how to give honor, and in addition, if dishonor becomes evident, you can recover and let the renewal of the spirit work within your life.

Rachelle Green (Sister of Author)
Hall Coordinator
Southern University A&M College
Baton Rouge, LA

In a society where we fail to understand the importance of faith in God, I believe we must open our eyes and heart to honor again. We are in an age where many have been blinded from paying tribute to the legends of faith, pioneers of movements, leaders, people of transformation, and communities who have fought spiritually and emotionally for the importance of their purpose and place in destiny. We all have felt misplaced and unseen as the sacredness of love, grace, and honor has begun to die. I encourage you to stand firm in your journey and remain steadfast in your calling. We must rekindle the Honor Code.

It's my great pleasure and honor to have my shoulder side by side with Dontrell Green, a great friend, trusted companion, and prophetic revolutionary. Within the pages of his book, you will find the passion to pursue the purpose in honoring. I know this book will open your eyes, bless your heart, and equip your spirit.

Apostle Daniel Emerson
Founder of ATR Global Ministries
Alexandria, LA

I've had the great opportunity to witness the growth of Prophet Dontrell Green. Honor has allowed him to rise to a place of prominence and stature. When I think about his growth, I'm reminded of Luke 2:52 which says, "…and Jesus (prophet Green) grew in Wisdom, Stature and Favor with God and man." Prophet Green as the Lord continues to enlarge your territory, always remember you can't "stand on TOP of" what you don't "Understand". UNDERstanding is the Posture of Honor!

Apostle Shannon Comery Sr.
Founder of Men Touring LLC
Author of Though It Tarry
Zachery, LA

FOREWORD

The principle of honor is one of the greatest foundational principles that's mentioned throughout scripture. Biblically the word honor can be defined as, "the state of being highly respected or revered." Since the beginning of creation, it has always been God's will, that humanity lives life in a way that produces high respect and reverence to God. Unfortunately, because of the fall of man through the sin of Adam, God's perfect creative order was corrupted. This corruption resulted in the principle of honor being lost, distorted, and in some instances even perverted. As a result of these negative effects of sin, mankind began to dishonor God in many ways, which can be seen through the various forms of idolatry that are mentioned in the Bible. Men would begin to honor themselves as gods as opposed to honoring the True and living God, Yahweh. Men would begin to place their hope in their own resources, riches, talents, and abilities, which would result in a culture that is now governed by humanistic reasoning and secular philosophy that is anti-Christ in nature. It is for this reason that God has released a clarion call into the earth, that is designed to awaken His people to the reality that reformation and the restoration of honor is of vital necessity.

Prophet Dontrell Green Sr. is one of the voices that God has raised to initiate a work of reformation that will restore God's original order regarding the principle of honor. In his book, "The *Honor Code*", he addresses many cultural manifestations of dishonor, while simultaneously revealing God's plan and purpose for honor. *"The Honor Code"* serves as a divine manuscript that contains the revelatory power to bring alignment into the hearts of men concerning the interworking framework of the principle of honor. "*The Honor Code"* provides the reader with a step-by-step scriptural guide that serves as a means of empowerment in the life of the reader. The principles that are conveyed in this book, can be applied cross-culturally in a way that converges various cultures to God's perfect will. These principles can be applied to various systems and institutions such as marriage, family, government, church, and the workforce. These same principles embody contextual application that can be applied to various relationships and spheres of influence in the earth.

I highly recommend that all believers purchase a copy of this book and apply the principles of this book to their lives. I would encourage leaders in a ministerial capacity to also purchase this book as well. The wisdom and insight that the "*Honor Code*" contains, can serve as a vital asset that can assist in the building process and establishment of honor-based cultures. The establishment of biblically based cultures of honor is of the utmost importance in this day and age as cultures shape societal frameworks. The wealth of knowledge that this book carries has the potential to bring correction, clarity, insight, and strategy that can be applied to individuals, teams, and systems abroad. As you read this book, I encourage you to approach it with an open mind and an open heart to receive the revelation that God desires for you to obtain through these writings. Prepare yourself to receive the transformational power of "*The Honor Code*"!

APOSTLE STEVEN HALLIBURTON
LEAD PASTOR OF THE BROOKPLACE
CLARKSVILLE, TENNESSEE

INTRODUCTION

More than ever, we are at a time and season where we need honor restored in the world and most importantly, in the body of Christ. It seems as if many would rather dishonor than to really show real, genuine honor to one another, yet they find it easy to gossip, slander, ridicule and tear each other down. Honor isn't just something you throw around or say loosely but is earned and rewarded to those who know what it means to be honored and how to show it. This book, "The Honor Code" will help you gain your honor back and help you maximize your honor for others in a deeper depth for greatness and success in all spheres of life. Honor is lacking and we need desperately a culture that knows how to honor with integrity and humility. One of the ways you achieve honor or considered to be honorable is how you honor and reverence God. The Bible clearly says all honor and glory belongs unto God (Revelation 7:12). This is the beginning of a maximized life full of honor by honoring one who is far beyond greater than you. Did you know that honor is a realm or perhaps a dimension? And there are key principles on entering this realm with God. Yes, you can receive keys & codes to unlock a sustainable lifestyle of honor in every area of your life. Honor is the premise of a life of blessings and longevity. I remember August of 2019, back home at my family church; we were headed to go give our greetings to the pastor of the church because it was his birthday celebration. Upon approaching him, he said, "come here, my son!" And as I got ready to move closer towards him, he began to somewhat speak a word of encouragement unto me saying: "because you honor God, you will be blessed in every aspect of your life". When he spoke those words to me, they begin to take root within me and unlock something on the inside of me that I will never forget because it was then I had found a key to a life of blessings. In that moment, I understood it wasn't just about works nor just in words alone, but honor is something that develops deep within, and God cares more about you honoring him than anything else. Since then, I've been on a journey, to learn more about honor and how I can walk more in it to be able to help the next generation and become a distributor of it. The Bible makes mention of the word honor 147 times throughout the Bible. This means honor is pretty big to God and there is no other way around it. The word honor can be described as to: "hold to high respect; great esteem, to reverence, give glory or of great importance and notability. When we are talking about honoring a person, place, or thing, these are the measures we are taking to show and give. Another reason for writing this book is to provide you with the language of honor, but also the awareness of knowing how to receive it, when it's being shown, and when given. Don't you know that when you honorothers, God in return honors you? Honor is the foundation in which things can be established and the one thing that holds relationships together and lasting. In heaven, the angels of the lord have one job and it's to worship, praise, give glory, and honor.

> 13 And every creature which is in heaven, and on the earth, and under the earth, and such as are in the sea, and all that are in them, heard I saying, Blessing, and honour, and glory, and power, be unto him that sitteth upon the throne, and unto the Lamb for ever and ever.
>
> 14 And the four beasts said, Amen. And the four and twenty elders fell down and worshipped him that liveth for ever and ever. **(Revelation 5:13-14 KJV).**

Do you see the point? Honor is imperative and if the angels in heaven can do it, so can you. When you're truly walking in the posture of honor, those around you will recognize it and the honor you possess will become contagious. The objective of honor is to attract; so that it will bring impact to the lives around you and the world at large. The honor God is calling many of you to walk in will be like a fragrance and you will carry it everywhere you go, causing great doors to open and giving you the ability to gain prestige as well as a great influence. There is such a favor that comes when you honor, that it commands men on earth and in heaven to look upon you. Honor isn't just something you grow into, but you're born with it, and you gravitate towards it. So much so that Jesus' birth caused wise men and shepherds to come unto his beckon (Matthew 2:1-11). The honor and majesty he arrayed on earth two thousand years ago attracted and made him like a magnet at a great remoteness. You too possess this honor in you when you accepted Jesus Christ as your Lord and Savior. It is in your DNA and every time you show honor; you show a little of who Jesus is to the world. This book will impart wisdom into you concerning how to retrieve honor and live it out. This 21-day pathway will give you new codes and abilities to cultivate those around you and give you the attitude to always want to remain honorable. May honor be laced in your heart and may this knowledge of it plant big seeds of abundance.

-Whoever pursues righteousness and kindness will find life, righteousness, and honor. **Proverbs 21:21 ESV**

DAY 1

"Honor Your Home"

So, whether you eat or drink or whatever you do,
do it all for the glory of God.

1CORINTHIANS 10:31 NIV

One morning I woke up getting ready to start my day and as I began to move around my home, I realized that it needed some attention (cleaning). At that moment, I was getting frustrated because I had so much on my plate to do that day, but I knew I could not ignore it or start my day off the proper way without first tending to my home. As I began to doubt myself and throw somewhat of a tantrum as if I was a two-year-old whose lollipop was taken away; I was touched by the Holy Spirit in such a peaceful way and heard his voice in the midst of wanting to give up. I heard him clearly say "honor me with your home!" And suddenly, I could feel the tangible presence of God and was overcome with his peace. He then began to reveal to me the importance of honoring your home. Many times, we fuss and complain about the home God has given unto us and never take the time to think about those who are less fortunate and who have no home or those who may not be privileged to afford the home you have. This revelation was the wisdom I needed, and it made me appreciate more the blessing of the home God has given me. It caused me to be thankful, give glory, praise, and honor unto God for all he had done for me and my family. Did you know that when we clean and cherish the things in our home, we honor God? Indeed, we do, because you are showing God you are grateful for what he has given unto you and it shows you are a good, capable steward of the blessings he has bestowed upon you ("His lord said unto him, well done, good and faithful servant; thou hast been faithful over a few things, I will make thee ruler over many things: enter thou into the joy of thy lord." Matthew 25:23 KJV).

Quite often we risk the danger of complaining more than giving thanks and it limits God from continually blessing us. Right within this encounter, I began to worship God, repent of my ungratefulness, and clean. I also knew this was an opportunity as well as an invitation for God to mature and mold me. One thing I learned about God is that He uses our circumstances to shape us and teach us, at all costs.

Make a Tabernacle

"Make this tabernacle and all its furnishings
exactly like the pattern I will show you" **Exodus 25:9 NIV**

Now, knowing this truth of keeping my home clean with God and that it would bring honor unto him, I was hit with another revelation which we should all be mindful of and take into consideration in our home; we must make sure to welcome him into our home. We all should be eager and persistent in inviting him in. He comes in and dwells with us when He is invited, (Revelation 3:20). I've noticed over the years that if you're going to get a visitation from God, you must be willing to set up a tabernacle for him and invite him. In acts such as these they are honorable towards God, and it causes your home to be endowed with open heaven rewards. This is the same thing that took place in the life of Obed-Edom when David gave charge for the ark of the covenant to be placed in his home.

"He was not willing to take the ark of the Lord to be with him in the City of David. Instead, he took it to the house of Obed-Edom the Gittite. [11] The ark of the Lord remained in the house of Obed-Edom the Gittite for three months, and the Lord blessed him and his entire household" (2 Samuel 6:10-11 NIV).

How honorable was that to have the Ark of God Almighty sitting in his home with him and his entire family. He was able to reap the benefits of heaven for three months because he was graced and favored by the king at such a pivotal time. It is with great honor to host the presence of God because we are assured to know Him in a deeper intimate way and receive of His wisdom as well as His goodness. This is why it is important we guard our homes and are very careful of what we allow in our homes; what we say and listen to in our homes. Honoring God with our home means making sacrifices so that he can take habitation with us and live among us. When the presence of God lives in our homes, no sickness, death, or confusion can come in, and nothing goes undone. Your home is a gateway for God to come in, so honor him with it.

> So I have gazed upon You in the sanctuary, To see Your power and Your glory. Because Your lovingkindness is better than life, My lips shall praise You. **Psalms 63:2-3 AMP**

DAY 2

"Remaining Honorable"

43 "You have heard that it was said, 'Love your neighbor[i] and hate your enemy.'
44 But I tell you, love your enemies and pray for those who persecute you, 45 that
you may be children of your Father in heaven. He causes his sun to rise on the
evil and the good, and sends rain on the righteous and the unrighteous

MATTHEW 5:43-45 NIV

Many occasions can arise to cause us to discontinue to honor those we hold in high regard but no matter the situation or circumstance, it's imperative we remain honorable. True honor is proven when

you can still maintain your stand even in the midst of criticism, persecution or when someone errs. Can you remain honorable in these tough times? This is the question we should all acquaint ourselves with, ask ourselves in trying times and be reminded of. However, this comes from a lifestyle totally dedicated and surrendered unto the Lord. When you truly carry the heart of the father you will not allow the smallest of things to creep into your heart. A lot of times when we find ourselves not continuing to be honorable it is because we lack love and mercy or don't know how to forgive. ("Blessed are the merciful, for they will be shown mercy. Blessed are the pure in heart, for they will see God". Matthew 5:7-8

NIV). Of course, what they've done hurts and I'm not saying be numb about it but don't allow what happened to take the place of honor because there is a reward for your faithfulness and your commitment. I can recall when I was going through a tough season of transition in finding a church home and some people were so sure I wouldn't make it and that I wasn't going to amount to anything. They had left me high and dry, leaving me and my ministry to die all because of a disagreement. They had turned their backs on me, and I cried many nights and wanted to give up. I wanted to give them a piece of my mind, but I also remember the voice of the Lord kept saying to remain honorable. You would think after they had done these wrong things, I would have the right to approach them or in return do the same thing unto them, but that's not so because God gets no glory in your retaliation. Many times, God would allow a thing for your protection, to humble you, and to stretch you for your next level. See, in that season, God was challenging me to remain honorable because I was going to need it for where I was going. You don't have to fight vengeance with a vengeance because it's theLord's battle (Romans 12:19 NIV). In fact, your honor causes God to move swiftly on your behalf to vindicate, rescue, and compensate. In addition, this was the same measure David took when Saul was pursuing him in the books of 1 Samuel and 2 Samuel. ([5] Afterward, David's [a]conscience bothered him because he had cut off the hem of Saul's *robe.* [6] He said to his men, "The Lord forbid that I should do this thing to my master, the Lord's anointed, to put out my hand against him, since he is the anointed of the Lord" 1Samuel 24AMP).

David understood the principle of honor and because of this, his house reigned forever. Unfortunately, it has been a struggle for very many in this generation to grasp and come to grips with. There is a lot we can learn from David here. For one, he had a conscience and took responsibility for his actions. Secondly, he was considered one of God's anointed. Maybe you've been in a situation where you wanted to get back at someone anointed by

God. I would advise you to reconsider and use the example of David, because in doing so you will see the favor and the hand of God intervene.

Guard Your Mouth

It is also wise to guard your mouth in these times of persecution whether behind closed doors or when in conversation with others. All of this opens the door to dishonor and causes you to become dishonorable. In fact, you should allow these moments to settle your heart, positioning yourself to learn more about how to pray for those who violated you. Your mouth is a weapon and when your emotions are under attack, it becomes a weapon of the enemy to sow seeds of dishonor, sabotage, and discredit. We should be slow to speak and swift to listen (James 1:19 NIV). The enemy knows if he can cause you to become bitter after a betrayal, then he can manipulate you into being dishonorable, but I hear the Lord today telling you to REMAIN HONORABLE! Remember to remain honorable in words and in actions, and watch God do his part.

> [8] *but no human being can tame the tongue. It is a restless evil, full of deadly poison.*
>
> [9] *With the tongue we praise our Lord and Father, and with it we curse human beings, who have been made in God's likeness.* [10] *Out of the same mouth come praise and cursing. My brothers and sisters, this should not be.* **James 3:8-10NIV**

PRAYER

As you've read on this subject today, I pray that you will gain a grace to endure and leverage to face all odds no matter what may come your way and I declare that what seems to be an attack will turn in your favor. I decree you will always and forever remain honorable because you understand its importance and because you love God just that much. This is my prayer in Jesus' mighty name.

DAY 3

"DISHONOR"

If you do not listen, and if you do not take it to heart to give honor to My name, " says the Lord of hosts, "then I will send the curse upon you and I will curse your blessings; and indeed, I have cursed them already, because you are not taking it to heart.

MALACHI 2:2 ESV

It doesn't take a whole lot to be honorable, but it takes more to be dishonorable. Yes! It takes more to be dishonorable. In fact, I've never understood why so many would go to certain extents to just dishonor when all they had to do was simply honor. Dishonor is considered a sin in the eyes of God, and you do more harm than good when you dishonor. The blessings of God cannot reside in a person who purposely chooses to dishonor. Webster describes dishonor as: "a state of shame or disgrace." Another way of explaining dishonor is; failing to observe or respect. It is humiliating and disgusting. See, every time we decide to dishonor, we are doing the opposite of who God has called us to be. As children of God, we should reflect the father by showing honor. However, when we dishonor, the face of God is moved from us, and we are not able to progress in life as we would like or how God desires for us. As I look out over the landscape of the earth, I see so much dishonor and it literally grieves the heart of the Father. If I had to describe dishonor in my own words; it is the seed bed of; pride, rebellion, betrayal, and deceit. When you dishonor, you not only disgrace God but you also betray him because you are doing the opposite of what he has commanded you to do. Dishonor opens the door to pride and as you know pride is an abomination unto God (Proverbs 16:5). This was the same attack that caused Satan to be cast down from heaven and even Saul in the Old Testament to have his kingdom torn from him. When we fail to show honor, we fall into these snares, and some never recover. However, the more you honor, the more dishonor becomes unfamiliar to you. You will not have the stomach for it, and you become an alien unto it. Let's look at the story of Saul, king of Israel and examine some of the characteristics he showed as it relates to dishonor.

THE DISHONORABLE KING

In the book of 1 Samuel, we see a king who is chosen by the people rather than by God and is anointed to be the first king of Israel in the monarchy age. Saul is no question or of doubts a king that many would have considered to be fit for the job. He was among the prophets and even prophesied when the Spirit of God came upon him. He even led Israel into many battles of victories but remember it's not how you start but how you finish. Saul's reign as king started good and continued until he could not follow a simple instruction from the Lord. He allowed his own will to get in the way of what the Lord had commanded. ([10] Then the word of the LORD came to Samuel, saying, [11]I regret that I made Saul king, for he has turned away from following Me and has not carried out My commands." Samuel was angry [over Saul's failure] and he cried out to the LORD all night" 1Samuel 15NIV). From this text, we can see that dishonor will cause God to become angry with you and have regret concerning you. That's why we must do a thorough job of examining ourselves daily to make sure that we do not allow the spirit of dishonor to enter our lives. Dishonor will cause years of hard work and labor to come tumbling down when it's placed in the hearts of those who lack honor. Saul's labor became vain to God because he had failed to grasp this concept. Don't allow this to be you, but rather appreciate to honor those God has placed among you. In a season where God desires to truly bless you, don't let him find dishonor in you. However, let your cup overflow with integrity and honor.

> But now thou hast cast us off, and brought us to dishonor, And goest not forth with our hosts. **Psalms 44:9 ASV**

PRAYER

Father today I pray that dishonor will never be a hindrance in the lives of your people. I pray that they will learn the importance of honor and will divorce all forms of devices attached to dishonor. I pray they will not ever allow it to be in their hearts and I pray it will never be a blockage for the flow of their blessings in Jesus' mighty name. Amen.

DAY 4

"Honoring Your Marriage"

Let marriage be held in honor among all, and let the marriage bed be undefiled, for God will judge the sexually immoral and adulterous.

HEBREWS 13:4 ESV

Has it ever occurred to you that the reason many marriages are lacking intimacy, sustainability, communication, and growth is because of the lack of honor? Honor goes a long way and especially in marriage. In fact, marriage is one of the most precious things God takes honor in. Honor in your marriage reflects how you see God and how you honor Him. Marriage teaches us the importance of submission, commitment, and the power of agreement and covenant. When we are doing all these things in our marriage, it is a display and example of honor we show unto the father. Marriage is sacred and a powerful tool in the hands of God when two people align themselves together. Therefore, you must begin to honor your marriage and value it because it breaks the plans of the enemy over your life. Though some of you are yet to be married or perhaps may not have any ambitions of getting married, it is still imperative you understand the value and honor of marriage that you may not cross or access unauthorized areas of others' lives that are married.

I believe the reason why a lot of times we see confusion and lack of honor in this area is because many are afraid to admit the fact that they have not been cultivated in the area of honoring marriage in the way God sees it. Your marriage should be holy, pure, and only between you and your spouse (male & female). It is for this reason a man leaves his father and mother and holds fast to his wife (Genesis 2:24). Over the past decades, we have witnessed many divorces and separations in marriages because honor has waxed cold in many. However, as you begin to honor and hold your marriage in greater regard, you will see growth and progress. In your marriage, you should honor in your speech, in your actions, and your devotion to one another. The more time you spend with your spouse the better you will get to know them, and you will grow to honor them. You should love your spouse wholeheartedly and with great diligence. Your honor will likewise reflect your love for them and your reverence for them. Marriage should never be built on what one can get from the other, but it should be built on reciprocity, and one should always intend to give themselves unselfishly. In marriage, there is no little 'I' or 'you', but 'we': a partnership for a lifetime. Marriage will reveal the heart of one and give you details about yourself that you never thought was there because marriage teaches you principles in Christ that will reveal the heart of the Father. Honoring your marriage births honesty, humility, and excellence.

("Whoso findeth a wife findeth a good thing, and obtaineth favour of the LORD". Proverbs 18:22 KJV). See, when we find a spouse and honor that spouse, there is an undeniable favor that is released upon that marriage that will crack open mighty blessings and show forth the hand of God. Therefore, we should always honor our marriage and submit our marriage to God. In our marriage, Jesus should always be the center and we should submit to one another as the church has done unto Jesus (Ephesians 5:24). Honoring your marriage requires responsibility on all levels.

THE GOOD DAYS & BAD DAYS

Have you ever had a bad day in your marriage and you wanted to throw in the towel? Yes, I've had many of those and wanted many times to give up and call it quits. However, it's not the good days that are considered to be honorable unto God alone, but it's the days we stay and fight to make it through; that is honoring.

Have you ever wondered what we really mean when we say the vows for better or worse? In these vows, we are rendering our hearts unselfishly and are making a vow, that whatever happens we are anchored to stay at all costs. Good days or bad days should never reflect on your honor towards one another. In addition, God uses these moments in our lives to sharpen us and help us better understand one another. There must be a level of compromising and a level of understanding that goes beyond ones thinking but that will facilitate unity. Honoring your marriage is the key.

> 22 Wives, submit to your own husbands, bas to the Lord. 23 For the husband is the head of the wife even as Christ is the head of the church, his body, and is himself its Savior. 24 Now as the church submits to Christ, so also wives should submit fin everything to their husbands.
>
> 25 husbands, love your wives, as Christ loved the church and gave himself up for her, 26 that he might sanctify her, having cleansed her by the washing of water with the word, 27 so that he might present the church to himself in splendor, without spot or wrinkle or any such thing, that she might be holy and without blemish.1 28 In the same way husbands should love their wives as their own bodies. He who loves his wife loves himself. 29 For no one ever hated his own flesh, but nourishes and cherishes it, just as Christ does the church, 30 because I are members of his body. 31 "Therefore a man shall leave his father and mother and hold fast to his wife, and the two shall become one flesh." 32 This mystery is profound, and I am saying that it refers to Christ and the church. 33

However, let each one of you love his wife as himself, and let the wife see that she respects her husband. **Ephesians 5:22-33**

PRAYER

As we have come to a close, we cover all marriages and even those who are seeking to be married. We pray that marriages will be built on the foundation of God's word and that husbands and wives would learn to submit to one another and love one another no matter how hard life becomes. May marriages excel in strength and may the favor of God forever be with every married couple. In Jesus' matchless name. Amen

DAY 5

"UNLOCKING THE HONOR CODE FOR PARENTS"

Children, obey your parents in the Lord, for this is right. "Honor your father and mother," which is the first commandment with promise: "that it may be well with you and you may live long on the earth."

EPHESIANS 6:1-3 NKJV

Often, we hear the phrase "children are a gift from God". Well, so are parents because they are a part of making God's divine creation come into being. Parents are vital in the lives of their children especially in helping them become all that God has destined for them to be. Parents are your first form of authority on earth. Besides, your parents are a reflection of your Heavenly Father. They nurture, guide, love, and support in every area of your life. Parents take the extra mile and are considered to be safeguards. Therefore, it is very critical you honor them. They not only need honor, but they are deserving of the honor. It's not a matter of question or an opinion, but God commands us to honor them. It doesn't matter if they are good or bad, alive, or not, you are required to honor them because in doing so there is a reward, and it is honorable to God. I never grew up with my biological parents, in fact, my momma died when I was 2 years old,and I met my father at 17. However, no matter the circumstances, I still to this day honor and reverence my dad because I understand the magnitude of honoring your parents regardless of life uncertainties. I could have had many reasons not to honor him but remember there is no reward or longevity in dishonor. It's when we are truly crushed and when life throws us blows, we learn to mature and honor because everything is done for a reason. God made no mistake when he created you or decided to give you the parents he did. For God designed them just for you. He knew exactly what we needed and the parents that would have the grace and patience to be able to deal with us as well as the IQ so that we would be able to produce fruit and become successful. Another example or model we can follow is when Jesus Christ came into the earth with all power but did not execute power unless he first received permission from his father in Heaven (John 5:19). When we acknowledge and obey our parents, we honor them. In John chapter 5, we can see Jesus having much respect and honor for his Father because he understood the value of communicating with Him before doing anything. Therefore, the Bible states that if we honor our parents and obey them, our days here on earth with be longer. When honoring your mother and father there is protection. It shields you from danger and destruction. If Jesus never acknowledged or recognized his Father before making a decision, there is no telling what problem He would have faced during his time here on earth. Honoring your parents not only shows accountability, but also shows that you're a true son of God. It's a sign of submission and alignment and where there is order or unity, honor will flow.

> "A man who loves [skillful and godly] wisdom makes his father joyful, but he who associates with prostitutes wastes his wealth. **Proverbs 29:3AMP**

HAVING A HEART TO SERVE

Your parents' residue wisdom and experience can save you years of heartaches or pains. A mother cares for her child and a father strengthens his child. Without the balance of both facets, a son nor a daughter would be able to endure the weight of the world. If you follow these guidelines of honoring your parents, there is nothing you cannot achieve or become because God takes pleasure and is pleased when you obey your parents (Colossians 3:20). Of course, there will be times you don't see eye to eye, and you may not totally understand their reason for saying yes or no concerning some matters, but you have to comply with their request in any situation. You may never know what's in store on the other side, but if you obey, listen, and pay attention to honoring your parents, that could very well advance the plans and purposes God has for your life. How you honor your parents will reflect how you honor everyone else around you. God uses your parents to test you and teach you how to honor others outside of your place of familiarity. What you do at home will show in public so let's make it our business to honor all, starting with the ones who gave us life, our parents.

> "Listen to your father, who sired you, and do not despise your mother when she is old. Buy truth, and do not sell it; Get wisdom and instruction and understanding. The father of the righteous will greatly rejoices, and he who sires a wise child will have joy in him. Let your father and your mother be glad and let her who gave birth to you rejoice [in your wise and godly choices]." **Proverbs 23:22-25 AMP**

Another huge and major aspect of honoring your parents is serving them. Our parents should never have to ask us twice to do something, but we should eagerly and freely be willing to serve them. In serving them, we show honor and gratitude for the love and sacrifice they've made over the years. Where you serve, the blessings of God flow. This type of service to our parents establishes us for favor; a seed sown in which one day we will reap the same benefits. Honoring and serving our parents is one of the most important things we will ever do in life and that will never go unnoticed in the eyes of God. Honor your parents, it is your duty, and your future depends on it.

> A wise son makes a glad father, but a foolish man despises his mother.
> **Proverbs 15:20 ESV**

PRAYER

Dear Jesus, help us to better reverence and honor our parents. Teach us to respect, love, and serve them unselfishly and passionately. Jesus give us wisdom and never allow us to forget the sacrifice and labor of our parents. Help us to see them the way we see you and grace us with the power to raise a generation that will know what it truly means to honor their parents in Jesus' powerful name. Amen.

DAY 6

"Bring Honor to Your Workplace"

Whatever you do [whatever your task may be], work from the soul [that is, put in your very best effort], as [something done] for the Lord and not for men, knowing [with all certainty] that it is from the Lord [not from men] that you will receive the inheritance which is your [greatest] reward. It is the Lord Christ whom you [actually] serve.

COLOSSIANS 3:23-24 AMP

Everyone in life has been in a place where you want to blow up, erupt, and even want to tell the boss and customers off. I'll say you're not crazy but human. Have you ever questioned or wondered why you are on that job? I've been there many times and even thought of throwing in the towel a few times. Jobs sometimes can be so pressuring because you are forced to be social and must learn how to deal with colleagues and perhaps learn how to work with a team to get the job done. It's in these places God is training, grooming, and molding us for greatness. God is monitoring and testing us to see if we can handle being honorable in unfavorable or unpleasant environments and your workplace is a huge area. Often, we never take a moment to think about things such as our workplace being a vital place for us to display the glory of God and a place, we can bring honor to him. Honor is not measured by where, who, or what, but stretches beyond our reason, that it should and always bring glory to the father. Bringing honor to your workplace speaks volume and shows the maturity and character of one. It says you are integral and are willing to go the extra mile but also that you bear much fruit. Your workplace should be a place you show off the talents and gifts God has given to you and a place that, when men see you, they recognize the power of God at work in your life. As a believer of Jesus Christ, we have the power to shift atmospheres and therefore it's important we aim to bring honor to our workplace. No matter their status and belief or religion, honor everyone at work. Joseph, for instance, was sold into slavery by his brothers because he was favored by his father and in the midst of this horrible abuse, he never changed his stance on honoring those who were in authority over him. His first duty of work was when he was brought into Potiphar's house. The Bible states in Genesis 39:2-6 that everything Joseph touched prospered, so much so that Potiphar placed him in charge of all he owned. Consider this: when we have a heart of true service and honor, God will in return promote us and exalt us. It was in these moments in Joseph's life the glory of God was revealed, and Potiphar recognized that the Lord was with him. Joseph's diligence in the workplace could change the heart of his pagan master. See, your devotion in the workplace matters because just like Joseph you too can change the hearts and minds of your coworkers and managers. The place of business shouldn't affect your honor, yet it is important that you raise the bar. Joseph's honor unto God paid off because he did his work as it was unto God and because of this, the entire house of Potiphar was overtaken by the blessings of the Lord. I can recall a time in the year 2021 while on my job that I was able to display the glory of God by getting someone baptized. She was unaware of the message of the gospel or the importance of accepting Jesus Christ as her Lord and Savior. This experience shifted the trajectory of her life and her thinking because I was willing to not only talk the talk but also willing to live out a lifestyle of honor unto God even at my job. Honor is not just in speech but also in our actions and the workplace is one of the most vital places we can display honor without speaking as much. Your honor releases a fragrance in the atmosphere, and it shows within your performance. The way I was able to get my coworker saved was with my upbeat enthusiasm and passion for working, which opens a conversation of why I do what I do and why I'm always smiling, or why I do everything so orderly, honorable, or in excellence. This conversation opened a door to testifying of Jesus and the rest was history. Many times, there are those around you who are desperately in need to be uplifted and your honor in the workplace can be the very thing they need to shift their perspective on how they see their job. In the workplace, your labor is not in vain, God honors your labor, and nothing is a waste in His eyes.

Bringing honor to your workplace helps improve you as a person and allows others to see what it truly means to be a child of God. It also challenges them to do the same.

Your workplace is another major form of authority being placed in your life and how your treat authority reflects on how you govern as well as determine how you will survive throughout life and the real world. Your workplace is intended to supply financial stability. This is why it is imperative we don't mishandle ourselves on jobs or run off like a loose cannon. I was also told by a wise person that how you resign or retire is very important. Leaving honorably opens the door for new opportunities. In addition, did you know your honor can make you an employer? God can entrust you with your own when He sees how you treat, serve and honor another's possessions. He makes you the lender and not the borrower (Deuteronomy 28:12). Where you are faithful over the little, he will indeed make you ruler over much, and to whom much is given, much is required.

That much will always require your honor. Make it a habit to bring honor to your workplace.

> In the same way, let your light shine before others, so that they may see your good works and give glory to your Father who is in heaven. **Matthew 5:16 NIV**

PRAYER

Lord, today, we humble ourselves and ask that you make us better servants in the workplace, that we may bring glory unto your name. We pray for a heart that loves to help others. Give us leadership skills to be able to properly bring change into the marketplace. We ask for all these blessings in Jesus' name. Amen.

DAY 7

"Exemplifying Honor in The Land"

Let every person be subject to the governing authorities. For there is no authority except from God [granted by His permission and sanction], and those which exist have been put in place by God. Therefore whoever resists [governmental] authority resists the ordinance of God. And those who have resisted it will bring judgment (civil penalty) on themselves.

ROMANS 13:1-2 AMP

One of the most overlooked areas of honoring is knowing how to honor in the land. This means honoring your community, neighbors, law enforcement, firefighters, government, etc. If there has ever been a time in our history, we needed honor the most, now is the time. It is very critical today in the world that these principles and values be restored in our land so that we can look towards a better future and live in a land that is free of chaos, drama, and toxicity. Many times, we experience much chaos in our communities because of the lack of honor. It seems as if honor has been put on automatic pause and many go around having a poor way of showing it. Over the past decade and into the new one, I realize there have been more dishonor in the areas of our government, law enforcement and communities. For instance, if we would just learn to honor one another, we would see less crime, murder, racism, and political upheaval. Sadly, we live in a world where people only value their personal ambitions but cannot honor or respect the opinions of others. The question is; what has the world become? I grew up in a time when the entire neighborhood would help take care of you and a time when you could not pass up your neighbor's house without speaking or waving. Better yet, you couldn't even act up in school without everyone fussing at you or telling your momma. Cops weren't a threat but were safeguards around the community. Even though nobody cared for politicians, it still didn't stop the honor shown to them when they would go from door-to-door campaigning. See, this is when true honor is established and is exemplified in a land. Everyone gets along and everyone comes together for the greater good of the community, region, state, or nation. Dr. Martin Luther King Jr in the late 1960s when there was much racial discrimination in the land of America exemplified honor and humility by standing for unity and justice in the face ofviolence. That's exactly what we need today; a people who would stand for righteousness and enforce unity through the elements of honor. Dr. King understood the importance of honor despite his views towards corrupt democracy in the 1960s. He, however, never ceased to give honor and was able to help shape and bring reconciliation throughout an entire nation and impact the world at large. Today, we should follow the same example no matter our views on who is in what office, let honor be the solution. The Bible teaches us "...that requests, prayers, intercession, and thanksgiving be made for everyone for kings and all those in authority, that we may live peaceful and quiet lives in all godliness and holiness." (1 Timothy 2:1-2 NIV)

One of the major ways we can see a swift change in the land is by praying for our land and those who are in authority. We often focus more on what's wrong or what's around us when we can exemplify prayer as the solution. It is one of the leading forces behind change and transformation regarding touching the hearts of kings and nations. Esther, for example, shifted the entire kingdom of Israel when her people were under great persecution. She was a Queen who stood for justice and was able to turn the heart of the king with her boldness and confidence. Esther was a woman who recognized fasting and praying as a means to exhibit change and bring honor to her land (Esther 4:16). On numerous occasions, we quote the scripture in 2 chronicles 7:14 that says, "if my people, who are called by my name, will humble themselves and pray and seek my face and turn from their wicked ways, then I will hear from heaven, and I will forgive their sin and will heal their land."

However, the only way this scripture can be fulfilled is by first showing honor and humility. It takes true honor and humility to be able to humble yourself, repent and pray as well as have sincere honor for the one you're praying to, before you can see the proper healing take place in your land. Exemplifying honor throughout your land will require much sacrifice and precision to see peace and liberation. Nevertheless, this dimension of honor initiates that type of level of momentum in your land that is needed for change. Every day we awake, we should be on a quest to want to see honor implicated in our land because where there is goodness, there is productivity and a suitable place to take pride in. Let us not only see the honor in economic wealth or where everyone gets along and are called family. Exemplifying honor in your land brings safety, hope, joy, and love. Every act of honor and kindness impacts the whole land, and we should never take that for granted but should try our best to stay committed and devoted to always sowing seeds of honor. It's how you honor that you'll be remembered. The honor you betray in your land, marks you as a pillar throughout your land forever. Never forget your obligation and never miss the opportunity to show honor. It may influence your community for the kingdom of God, eternally.

I remain confident of this: I will see the goodness of the LORD in the land of the living. **Psalms 27:13 NIV**

PRAYER

Father, we give you glory and honor today and we say we love you. We declare that you will give us the heart and willingness to honor authority in our communities and we pray you would heal our land from selfish greed and corruption. We pray you would raise up pioneers to bring forth change and restore honor in the land, in Jesus' mighty name. Amen.

DAY 8

"Honoring Your Body"

Do you not know that your bodies are temples of the Holy Spirit, who is in you, whom you have received from God? You are not your own; you were bought at a price. Therefore honor God with your bodies.

MATTHEW 5:43-45 NIV

I woke up one morning and as I was sitting outside on the front porch, I began to look across the street from my house and I could see the kids playing in the park and having so much fun. Some were jumping, others were flipping and running. I then began to remember the times when I was in elementary school and began to ponder on how much energy we would burn by running and how healthy I was as a kid. It was during that moment I heard the Spirit of God say, "honor your body". Has it ever occurred to you that the reason there are a lot of health issues is because our bodies are not fit or in shape? However, to properly function in life, we need healthy bodies.

Your body should be honored by eating the right things, giving it the proper rest, and exercising it as often as you can. Not only that, but we should also see honoring our body as a means to please God. That means when we offer or dedicate our bodies unto God, it is no longer ours. We sacrifice our will and body so that He can dwell within us. Your body was molded and created by God almighty and it's important we take care of it. The Bible 'beseech you by the mercies of God, that ye present your bodies a living sacrifice, holy, acceptable unto God, which is your reasonable service' (Romans 12:1 KJV). In this scripture, Paul shows us the importance of presenting our bodies before God and what our bodies represent. He not only shows us key values of our body but also charges us to keep it holy and pure before the eyes of God. When you honor your body, you want to be that vessel that God can flow through. I can attest to this because as a prophetic voice, it is especially imperative, we consecrate our body to remain pure and fit for duty (Judges 13:3-5). Nevertheless, not only are you staying holy before God, but you should also honor your body because it's yours.

We live in a world where many do not take pride in what belongs to them, for some reasons, they have lost their sense of security for the things God has bestowed upon them and have fallen into a place of insecurity. Did you know one of the major causes of death is health issues in the body or not getting the proper nutrients needed? Another would be because of depression and mental illness. Therefore, you honor your body through the mind, soul, and of course the body itself. Your body is not to be overlooked or ignored, but as human beings, we should trust our body when it gives us signals that it is overly worked or fatigued. Our body will let us know if it's not getting the proper rest or food by shutting down or perhaps cramping and giving, such symptoms as headaches. When we are depressed or overwhelmed, the body will consume too much food, when the Bible clearly states not to overindulge (Proverbs 25:16 TPT). When we fully and intentionally honor our body, these are the things we must make certain to pay attention to and try our very best to avoid, so that we may have a healthy and long-lasting body.

Lastly, when our bodies are healthy, we also live longer and look younger. Having a healthy body rejuvenates your youth and makes you feel good about yourself. With a healthy body, you have more energy and can think.

Did you know that fasting helps you clearly hear the voice of God as well? Yes, fasting gives us the capability to hear from our creator and gives us an entrance into the spiritual world to be able to understand what God wants to do in the earth and in our lives. Fasting is another huge aspect of honoring your body and should always be considered if we are going to have a more intimate relationship with Jesus. The objective of honoring your body should not only be viewed in one way but in multiple ways to see the full potential of a healthy and suitable body. In addition, fasting is that area we need better equipping in, especially in today's world. It helps spiritually and physically. A good example is the story of Daniel who denied the king's food, preferring his. Daniel and his friends proved that their food was better nourished than any other young men who ate the royal food (Daniel 1:5-15). Living a lifestyle of fasting enables you a healthier life, but it is also honorable unto God. Daniel's act of obedience granted him, and his friends favor with the king's guard and God established Daniel with knowledge and understanding as well as interpretation of dreams and visions. His obedience to honor God with his body paved the way for him to be blessed and be able to stand up to authorities who were enforcing things outside the will of God. As you consider honoring your body in this season, I would also advise that you begin to discipline yourself and your body on fasting so that you will also see the results Daniel and his friends had in their time of trouble. Although they were dragged away from their homeland and everything was taken away from them, one thing remained: their devotion unto God and their way of communication. Fasting was their remedy and it sustained them all the days of their lives. Honor your body, for it will prove itself to be strong if you properly do what's needed.

That each of you should learn to control your own body in a way that is holy and honorable, **1 Thessalonians 4:4 NIV**

PRAYER

Dear Father, today, we ask that you give us the strength and endurance to keep our bodies pure and holy before you. We ask that we honor our body spiritually and physically by being very cautious on what we allow in and out. May you give us the grace to treat our bodies right and give us the appetite to fast and desist from unhealthy foods. Father, we pray for a renewed body, and we declare you are delivering us from the meat of the king's table. In Jesus' matchless name, Amen.

DAY 9

"Your Worship Signals Honor"

God is Spirit, and those who worship Him must worship in spirit and truth."

JOHN 4:24 NKJV

If we are going to truly bring honor throughout the earth, one of the ways we can do that is worship. Who or what you're worshiping matters because worship signals honor. That's why when we are worshipping, we must know exactly who we are doing it unto. The Bible makes it clear that "God is a spirit and those who worship him must worship him in spirit and truth" (John 4:24). This means worship should be done honorably because where there is truth, there will always be honor. Your worship is essential if you plan on honoring the almighty God. Your worship must be sincere. Worship is essential to a maximized life of peace and awareness. When you're in a place of worship, you are at the place of surrender and in awe of He who was, is, and is to come. Worship shows your true submissiveness and honor unto God. This is why we should never miss an opportunity to worship. I love the story of the lady at the well. In John chapter 4, we see a lady who was broken, thirsty, and desperately needed saving. In the context of the story, we find that she understood the importance of honoring; she had knowledge of her nation's background (history). She begins to state in verses 9 to 12 of John chapter 4 that she was not supposed to give Jesus water due to her cultural custom because He was a Jew (she honored and respected the Jewish protocol). She then goes on to reverence her founding father, Jacob who had dug the well, that they were fetching from. I believe her diligence in following and honoring protocol is what caused her to experience a true breakthrough. See, there is a reward when you honor those who have gone before you and have laid the foundation from which you are benefiting. Never miss the opportunity to honor those who have sacrificed for you. The Samaritan woman had the code of honor despite her circumstances.

Next, we see in the scriptures where Jesus ministers unto her about drinking water, and those who drink this water (of him) will not thirst any longer. Jesus was referencing that He was the water that she had longed for; the one she truly needed to drink. The water of Jesus brings eternal life. The woman understood she had no need to search anymore and asked him to give her that water. In the midst of this transaction, she realizes she was before a prophet because He asks her to bring her husband, knowing that she was not married to a man and because of her honesty during this conversation, it was honorable in the eyes of Jesus. This opened the door of her breakthrough. Our transparency reflects and attracts the honor of God. This is also what true worship offers (the liberty to be transparent). However, this lady was a sinner, but because she thought to be truthful, it proved to be honoring. Later, we find in this story that she was curious to how. She knew it was the custom of the Jews during that time to worship on the mountain of Jerusalem in the temple but being a Samaritan, she could not. Jesus tells her something so profound; "those who worship me must worship me in spirit and in truth," which indicates that our worship is not based on a geographic location, but should reflect how we sincerely love

Jesus. We shouldn't just worship because we are at a certain place or because people are watching, but we should worship at any given moment. True Honor unto God is what you do when nobody is looking. Can you worship when no one is looking or forcing you? I remember there have been times in church services when the preacher or worship leader must take hours to exalt to get people in the congregation to worship. When it shouldn't have to take all these measures. When you truly honor God, it doesn't matter who is looking or perhaps where you are, but you will stop wherever you are and worship him. Many fail to worship outside of their Sunday service and that is the reason why they lack honor and why their lives are in turmoil. Worship is not a one-time thing but it's a daily offering before the throne of God. Through your worship, we should lift our hands, clap our hands, stomp out feet and even bow our heads before God. All these postures signal our honor towards the father, in and throughout our ability to worship. Recently, I was at a concert where many gathered to worship and in the auditorium, you could feel such a beautiful presence of God's glory because everyone within the concert hearts was postured to worship and had no pride in withholding anything from the almighty God. When we worship, we must be willing to withhold nothing and must fully yield our hearts to see the purity of worship and the results we are seeking. We must be willing to express our intimacy unto the father unashamed. If we look at the life of David, we see that this is exactly what he did to give worship and honor unto God by dancing as a king, naked, before his people (2 Samuel 6:14-22). Worship is essential to the life of a believer, and it is very vital in our way of honoring God. That is why we should never take for granted the opportunity to raise our hands, clap them, etc. because it is one of the key roles of showing honor. David even mentions in Psalms 24 how he will always bless the Lord and his praises will continue to be in his mouth. In this Psalm, the writer is showing and referring that his words are in association with his worship and praise unto God, which reflects his honor.

This is the same kind of worship we all should embrace if we are striving for a lifestyle of honor and intimacy with the father. Worship shouldn't be reactive, but something proactive that stirs the inside of the believer. Today as you reflect on this pathway, I challenge you to worship God with your lips and with your utmost being. I challenge you to find a time where it's just you and the father, that you may go and sit before him training yourself how to posture before him and worship. Let today be the day you advance in your honor towards the father and become intimate with him by releasing a sound in the earth that signals a true sign of honor and reverence. You can start today with your worship.

> I will give thanks and praise the Lord, with all my heart; I will tell aloud all Your wonders and marvelous deeds. I will rejoice and exult in you; I will sing praise to Your name, O Most High. **Psalms 9:1-2 AMP**

PRAYER

Father, today we declare that as your people have read about worship, you will restore their passion for worship and make them vessels that worship on a daily basis. I pray that you will give them the heart to worship and that you will inscribe songs of worship upon their hearts. May all that they do be honoring unto you and may worship become the breath they breathe and live. In Jesus' precious name. Amen.

DAY 10

"Staying Honorable to Your Commitments"

Commit to the Lord whatever you do,
and he will establish your plans.

PROVERBS 16:3 NIV

I believe another huge and most overlooked area of honor in the world is commitment. Rather it be on a job, writing a book, being in relationships, attending a family function, etc. we devalue and lack commitment. Which indicates we don't honor our commitments. We say one thing but do another or in some cases, nothing at all. This has become a huge problem and barrier in many lives, leaving them in a place of delay and stagnation because they fail to honor their previous commitment.

When we fail to keep our commitments, it is dishonorable before God, and it shows the level of our focus but also that we can't be trusted. Many would say different but what's the difference between a lie and a commitment not fulfilled? They both show our inability to stay true to our agreements or our word. I found, over the past few years, that many are frustrated or angry because someone failed to keep a commitment made unto them or a word they gave. Many were told a lie or given an unfilled promise. However, God wants to reestablish our commitments because when we stay true to them, it brings honor unto his name as well as our reputation. The Bible makes it clear that "A good name [earned by honorable behavior, godly wisdom, moral courage, and personal integrity] is more desirable than great riches; And favor is better than silver and gold (Proverbs 22:1AMP). Has it ever occurred to you why many around the world can't get a loan from the bank and some can? It's because they have a track record of either not keeping their word of making their payments and others having the ability to keep their word, which qualifies them for perfect credit scores (having favor everywhere they go). It is simply because they have the level of commitment and now their commitment has been credited unto them, that wherever they go they can get things sometimes without money. Wouldn't you want this type of reputation in the world, to be known as a person who keeps their word? I know I certainly would. Commitment gives you the ability to live a life free of regret. Many times, the reason why we have regret is because we keep wondering if and wishing without taking steps; 'if I would have done this; if I would have finished this; I wish I had stayed committed to that'. These are all the regrets our minds are entangled with when we fail to stay committed to a place or a thing. The Bible talks about a tree being planted by the rivers, that this tree will bear much fruit and prosper (Psalms 1:1-3). A life of commitment offers growth and prosperity. It enriches our life of stability and shows our accountability to that which we have given our yes to. Before we can truly be committed to anything, we first must make our commitment within our hearts. The mind can be made up but if our hearts haven't yielded, we will not see any results and we risk the chances of dishonoring the very thing we were called unto. A heart yielded unto commitment releases passion towards what's to be done (which enables hard work and dedication). Staying committed shuts out fear and doubts and adds to our faith and confidence. Staying committed gives us the reassurance that anything is possible, and nothing is impossible if we stay the course, no matter what may come our way. I remember one day while we were living in Louisiana, my wife and I were passing through a city in our hometown, she mentioned a moment she had as a young girl with commitment issues because she had experienced let downs. My wife instructed me to never tell a person I was going to do something if I'm not going to keep my word; she didn't want the same fate of our children. So, we enabled the code of commitment in our household and family, giving no chance to uncommitted people or issues to stand in the way of our success or destiny. I learned a valuable lesson that day to keep my word regardless of life situations and that our inability to stay committed to our word affects those around us. Although my wife had experienced hurt and rejection, she was able to gain wisdom and crack open another code of honor through her life experience that would in return help others around her and set her life up in a way to be successful because she understood the language of commitment. Jesus spoke about this in the book of Matthew chapter 5 where he explains to us to let our YES be YES and NO, NO. The scripture teaches us to keep the oath/commitments we make with/to others and show the importance of our yes or no. Often, we make promises we can't keep when we could have simply said no from the very beginning. We as human beings are afraid to say NO. We think if we say no, we are going to hurt someone's feelings or let someone down, but our inability to stay committed to our yes causes more harm than good. There is power in our no as well as it is in our yes. In our no, it gives and offers those around us the chance to seek help elsewhere and the opportunity to alter their decision. It saves them time and energy but also shows our humility, honesty, and honor towards their situation. Never feel intimated by your 'no' concerning someone, there is always someone else better for the job or available. However, your yes will either advance others or hinder them. Therefore, your commitments are highly imperative. As you step on to this pathway today, I would encourage you to examine your commitments and ask yourself this question: Have I been true and dedicated to my previous commitments? If the answer is no, then allow the Spirit of God to renew your heart and mind and go back full of wisdom, knowing you have committed your ways unto the Lord. Always remember that staying committed is a way of showing and being honorable. In this book, I'm committed and dedicated to helping you improve your commitment and honor. It is my duty to you, so that you become better than what you ever were before.

> Delight yourself in the Lord, And He will give you the desires and petitions of your heart. Commit your way to the Lord; Trust in Him also and He will do it. **Psalms 37:4-5 AMP**

PRAYER

Father, today, we commit our will and ways unto you, asking Lord that you will give us the focus as well as the ability to stay committed to things we have taken an oath to. Father, we pray you allow us to be at peace with our yes or no and give us peace with any decision we make, knowing with you, all will be well. Allow us to remain true to ourselves and give us the confidence to stand in the midst of adversity. Let all we do be honoring unto your name and make us more like you. In Jesus' matchless name. Amen.

DAY 11

"Honor With Your Giving"

Honor the Lord with your wealth And with the first fruits of all your crops (income); Then your barns will be abundantly filled And your vats will overflow with new wine.

PROVERBS 3:9-10 AMP

Since I was a child; I've always had this desire to want to help everybody. I never understood it, but I always found myself giving whether it was food, money, clothes, my time, or even my heart, etc. I was determined

to give and was unaware of its benefits or rewards. I just knew it was the right thing to do. As I have gotten older, that same determination is still here today. So much so, I probably give a little over the board, but there is never too much giving when your heart is in the right place. I've realized that my giving shows honor, my compassion, and my concerns for others. There is nothing more joyful and honorable unto God when he sees that we give not only to Him but when we look out and think about others. It shows we are reasonable and not selfish or conceited. Did you know that when you give, it opens a doorfor others to give unto you? Yes, one of the key principles of the kingdom is giving. The Bible states give, and it shall be given (Luke 6:38). In the process of giving, there is an exchange like no other. Often, we look for others to give unto us when we haven't made a proper deposit. Don't worry, I've been guilty also once or twice in my life in moments of rock bottom which is actually the most important time to give because it shows where your heart truly is. Your giving has an advantage on your limited supply because when you sow, no matter what it is, you have an unchangeable promise that assures you that you will reap. Let's look at these covenant-keeping promises in God's word:

> "As long as the earth endures, seedtime and harvest, cold and heat, summer and winter, day and night will never cease. **(Genesis 8:22 NIV)**

> "Do not be deceived, God is not mocked; for whatever a man sows, this he will also reap. **(Galatians 6:7 NIV)**

These scriptures unfold everlasting promises God has sworn unto mankind, that if we sow, we can see a manifested blessing in return. It shows us the value of giving and the responsibility we have as believers and humans that we can't afford to disobey. When you give to the right place or right people, you are sowing into the kingdom of God. Your giving is associated with sowing and therefore for this reason this why you should make giving mandatory and a priority. Recently, while taking my family out to eat dinner, my 8year old son asked an important question. He said, "Dad, why does it say on the dollar bill "In God We Trust?" I politely answered him by saying because our nation (America) was founded on Christianity. With an unsettling answer in my heart, I began to ponder on this question the more, not fully knowing the answer but said my best at that moment. Then I heard the Lord say to me to honor Him with my giving. Although it was about money, we can still use this principle on any measure of giving.

Has it ever come to your attention God gave us a message to trust him with our money? I was blown away with this revelation because for years I had been seeing this quote on our nation's money but in that moment, I had finally got the message it was imitating; that if we trust God with our money, then when we give, we can trust that he will in return give back unto us and supply our very needs. I also began to research money and learned money is a currency which is understood to be a continuous flow, traction, or distribution. When we have money, it is not intended to be kept forever, but it is meant to be given, to see more come in. It is the same way with the laws of God, the same rule applies. Giving is such a big aspect in the kingdom of God, that God himself gave his only begotten son to die for all humanity (John 3:16) and who then, became the redeemer of the world. How much more wouldn't you want to give? It should be volunteered as well as cheerful and never in hopes of gaining something in return, but from the heart and not grudgingly.

> *So let* each one *give* as he purposes in his heart, not grudgingly or of necessity; for God loves a cheerful giver. **2Corinthians 9:7 NKJV**

There is no joy in giving when it is demanding or pressuring because God does not acknowledge honor under those circumstances. However, you should always seek him on how he would like for you to give. For some of you, God is looking for you to give your time, others give your food and many others he is looking for you to give a "YES" again. Maybe you stopped giving because someone tried to take advantage of you or maybe you lost the joy in giving. Whatever the case may be, don't stop giving because it is honoring and pleasing unto the father. Yes, I've heard the usual story of "they trying to get over on me or they don't need my help", on many occasions. Yeah, I've been down that road, but it doesn't excuse us from giving because we have a standard to live by once we've accepted Jesus Christ as our personal Savior, and once we've truly understood the true importance of honor.

The magnitude of your giving shouldn't be to a particular people as well as who you like or who you would rather show favor. Giving should be done in honor unto all, no matter how big or small. I find it strange that some people believe that to get favor with God, they must give to a special person or that their giving should be publicized. The Bible clearly lets us know that whatever we do should be done in secret (Matthew 6:30). Many miss their breakthrough trying to give unto well-known names and skip over people that are truly in need, but when you give in secret, God blesses openly and if you chose to refuse in giving, your hands will remain empty. Taking the moment and opportunity to give to that person that is poor or homeless is just as important to that mother who needs to pay her light bill. They both matter and eagerly need your help. So, when givers show up on the scene, they become the beacon light unto their darkness and the solution unto their problem. God sees this and the kingdom of heaven rejoices because you decided to stand in the gap and make a difference with your giving that will change the trajectory of another's life. Never hesitate to give and be willing, knowing that if you do, you will eat the good of the Land. You can start today and continue for the rest of your life by honoring with your giving. You've been created to give and to be a hero in a time of need. Never assume others don't need but always be ready to lend a hand because you could be the prayer they've been waiting on their entire life.

> He who has pity on the poor lends to the Lord, And He will pay back what he has given. **Proverbs 19:17 NKJV**

PRAYER

Dear heavenly Father, we come before you today asking and praying that you help us in the place of giving and ask father that you will put us in a better place to give. We pray that we will not see the face but rather that we would see the need and that you will supply our every need. Lord, we ask for a heart and mind of giving and that you will change our perspective today on giving and that we will not see it as a curse, but as a blessing to push your kingdom forward. In Jesus' matchless name. Amen.

DAY 12

"Celebrating Others Reflects Honor"

Rejoice with those who rejoice;
mourn with those who mourn.

ROMANS 12:15 NIV

A vital element of honor is being able to celebrate others without any resentment or motive but being able to unselfishly celebrate others as they succeed in life. This is what true honor is all about. It is hard to find those who are willing to put themselves to the side to affirm and celebrate the lives of others as well as being truly happy for another's success. However, when one is found celebrating the success of another individual, it reflects the honor of heaven. The Bible is clear when it lets us know the importance of rejoicing with those who rejoice and mourn with those who mourn but I've found over the years that people would rather mourn over others versus rejoice with and celebrate them. We are in a culture and generation where many hearts are hardened, bitter, and are envious of one another. Nevertheless, I've learned that it is not wise to covet another, but rather we should pursue in honoring and celebrating those who have worked hard and diligently in becoming successful in any area of their lives or perhaps in receiving any blessing or endeavor. What you make happen for another shall surely happen for you. Did you know it takes more energy being jealous of someone than to celebrate? Yes, it doesn't take much to cheer someone on or even encourage them but to show no concern or happiness takes far more energy and shows the level of your maturity and the character of your heart. For instance, the prodigal son in the book of Luke 15:11 of the Bible, we learn of a man who had two sons and onewho asked for his inheritance before it was the time to receive it from his father. In his father's favor and grace, he grants his son with his heart's desire and his son goes on the journey to success and happiness or so he thought. However, the same son finds his journey a bit tougher than he thinks, spends all his money on reckless living and now is forced to work for a man who sent him to take care of his pigs. As the prodigal son is working one day, he finds himself desperately in need and hungry to the point he is willing to eat the pig's food. Thank God he came to himself! He goes back home unto his father and the father receives his son back with open arms and decided to give him a feast. Everything seems to be going well, everyone is happy and excited that he is home and safe but there is one problem. His other brother can't seem to look past his brother's past behavior and is so jealous he could not be happy for his brother who is finally home and is ready to make his wrongs right. This is a major problem in our world today because too often, we see this in the church and inhomes. Where you have those who are willing to celebrate with you no matter how bad you messed up or how many times you've failed, they will celebrate with you but then others want to hold you to your past and who are angry because you got the celebration and they were overlooked not understanding that their celebration can only come by way of humility, honor and celebrating others. This story of the prodigal son is a prime example of how we shouldn't respond when someone else is being celebrated. When we purposely decide not to celebrate others it grieves the holy spirit and frustrates the grace of God. One of the ways we represent and please God is by our love and care for others. Your celebrating is a way you show you care about people and that you are secure within your identity. Most people have a hard time celebrating others also because they are unsure of themselves or because they've never been truly celebrated, and they don't know how to show it. When you come into a community of others who lift each other and cheer one another on, it opens you up unto a reality of joy and peace and you too likewise will begin to celebrate others. Celebrating is contagious in the kingdom of God and should be implemented everywhere you go. It doesn't matter the magnitude of one's success or achievement, everyone should be celebrated and honored for their deeds as well as their service no matter what it looks like. Some celebrate birthdays, graduations, a new car, new homes, a promotion, etc. whatever the case may be, always remember your celebrating others reflects honor. This is a code we must begin to discover if we intend to see a life of abundance and if we seek to find favor in the eyes of the Lord. One of the highest forms of showing honor is through our celebration for others. It is considered to be pleasing and acceptable unto God. Rejoicing for someone else shows the level of our maturity, security, and confidence within ourselves. It's time to celebrate others.

> And so we celebrated because the Lord had indeed worked miracles for us. **PSALMS 126:3**

PRAYER

Father, today, I pray that you would give your people a heart and a passion to want to celebrate others. Today, we ask that you restore love and joy to your people and cause unity once more throughout families and believers. On this day, we look unto you who gives life, and we declare a season of celebration, laughter, and excitement in Jesus' precious name. Amen.

DAY 13

"Honesty Attracts Honor"

Kings are pleased when what you say is honest.
They value people who speak what is right.

PROVERBS 16:13 NIV

Honesty is a major characteristic of a leader and is something that should be held in high regard. Honesty is honored and valued among those who are noble and among those who hold seats of great power and authority. Your honesty shows your loyalty, that you are trustworthy and honorable. When you are honest, it transfers throughout generations after you and exemplifies the fruit of meekness. In the days we are living in, we all could use a little more honesty that will reflect the life of Jesus and that will set the stage for others to walk in. We are in a time where many are dishonest, deceitful, untrusted, and liars. An error that the Bible speaks of is here on earth. A great time of betrayal, rumors of war, false doctrine,etc. I believe through it all honesty can turn the tide and bring back honor unto the world. I believe that we lack honesty because many have been smothered by a lie and have had their shares of dishonesty and betrayal. However today God wants to set you free and open you up unto a life of truth and honesty that attracts honor. When I was growing up, I could recall my mother always telling me to tell the truth no matter how bad a situation may be or what it was I had caused because people are more drawn unto your honesty than a lie. The truth will always stand, but a lie will find you out. My mother would say honest people get a second chance, but a lie cannot go unpunished. What she was saying was your honesty brings about mercy, but an untruthful statement serves as a means of judgment. If I'm honest, no one wants to be around a dishonest person because a dishonest person can't be trusted and will lead you down a pathway of trouble and treachery. Those who are honest inherit wisdom and knowledge but those who are dishonest are handed a life of hardship and slavery. Did you know that when you tell a lie you must tell another lie just to maintain the first lie? Yes, funny right! There is no ending to the lies but when you are truthful there is nothing left to say but to remain integral and honest unto what you've spoken (Proverbs 11:3 MSG). It is my heart desire that we all come up higher in this hour concerning our honesty, rather on our job, in our marriage, on our taxes, in the courtroom, or perhaps as parents and citizens of the kingdom of God. We should all pursue and walk worthy of the call upon our lives, no matter the situation or circumstance. No one should aim or live from a double standard because a double-minded man is unstable in all his ways (James 1:8). Even double tongues are misleading and damaging. So, speak with honesty, act with honesty, and watch as the Lord favors you and as men honor you because once again, honesty attracts. When you participate in dishonesty, you have already become the fool and it makes you a coward in the face of truth. Honesty is the way to go and even if it means going low. Your character is more valued over any platform, material thing, or fame. Honesty brings about peace but the dishonest one can't sleep at night. I would rather have one honest person in my company than have a bunch of fools around me who lie. I remember journeying back home from Los Angeles from a trip of ministering and fellowship with a good friend of mine, my wife and I stopped at a gas station. I paid for the gas and then pumped, but I mistakenly went over. Although I was in a rush to get home and it was only 2 pennies over, I immediately went into the store to straighten out the matter, but the manager of the store told me not to worry about it and also thanked me for my honesty. As I got ready to hop back into the car to pull off, the same manager ran out of the store to continue to thank me and even went on to tell my wife she has a great husband who was honorable and honest. That day shaped my life tremulously because this was a stranger who valued the principle of honesty and because of my honesty, I was spoken highly of and granted favor although I went over with the gas. See, your honesty is not only needed in the public eyesight, but also in your private moments of life and among those who don't even know you. It made me realize that even when we think no one is looking, someone is always watching, and we must live a lifestyle honorable before the father. Before we can be honest with others, we first must be honest with ourselves. If we can't be truthful within ourselves, we will always fail to be truthful to those who seek our honesty. After my encounter at that gas station that day it has caused me to pray for greater grace in the area of honesty and never to be a disappointment even in private moments of life. The man at the gas station was attracted to my honesty and it moved him because in today's world it is very rare to find honest people. I'm glad I was able to be one out of a few who could be honest with something so small as two cents. Nevertheless, it doesn't matter how big or small the issue may be, your honesty at the end of the day is required at the forefront. It is the small things God is looking at and is testing us on, to see if we would be honest so that he can release more responsibility unto us and trust us. If we can't be trusted, we can't go higher. Therefore, your yield to be honest is going to be very important if you wish to obtain a maximum life of honor and success. Honesty attracts, but most importantly it attracts honor. May you advance in honesty and may you never bother again with a lie.

And you will know the truth, and the truth will set you free. **John 8:32 ESV**

PRAYER

Father, we ask that you give us the heart, mind, and will to live a lifestyle of honesty. Give us the courage to be truthful in the midst of adversity and give us peace as we follow your ways. Dear Lord, show us mercy and we repent of any lie or time we've been dishonest before you or with others. We ask that you restore us and help us to be honest from this day forward. In Jesus' Mighty Name, Amen.

DAY 14

"Honor Your Time"

Look carefully then how you walk, not as unwise but as wise, making the best use of the time, because the days are evil. Therefore do not be foolish, but understand what the will of the Lord is.

EPHESIANS 5:15-17ESV

A key aspect of becoming successful in life is predicated upon our time management and honoring that window of time that has been granted to us. Time is something one must not take lightly, and you should know it is very important in every area of your life. How you handle your time says a lot and who you give your time to is also very important. Many go through life wasting valuable time because either they don't understand its importance or they have the mentality that time is on their side, but this is not true, and one should be very careful of this type of thinking and with their time. When you are born into the earth, your time clock begins to run and your days on earth are numbered. In fact, time is so important unto God he created days and nights; a time in which we should be up and a time we should rest. He created seasons and spaces just so time could exist on the earth. Time is the essence in which we live to fulfill purpose and destiny, we should always make proper use of our time. On the earth, there are 24 times zones, 24 hours in a day, 7 days in a week, 52 weeks a year, and 365 days a year. That seems like a lot of time, right? Well imagine living today and gone tomorrow, we don't know the day nor the hour we will leave this earth and that is why we should never take time for granted and most importantly live with no restraint as well as to the full capacity, God has called for us to live. There have been times in my life when I have not been privileged to have the time to do certain things and I vowed that when I get the opportunity, I would get those things done and complete. How many times have you been in that position, asking God to give you time and when he did you came up with even more excuses and dishonored that time? We all have been there but now is the time God is saying honor your time because it's honorable and pleasing in his sight. Not only is honoring your time honorable, but it also reflects stewardship and discipline. It shows you are able to manage your time as well as value your time. Rather that is on your job, with your family, relationships, projects, etc. It is proven and accounted that you can manage your time. If we are not careful, we will waste our time on wrong things as it relates to too much TV, social media, in other people's businesses, in places we don't belong, etc. When we misplace our time, we either become idle or fall into sin. Having too much time on our hands can either hinder us or advance us, therefore we should make full use of our time. Those who take time for granted never become successful nor do they ever see any progress or produce any fruit in their life. If you ever become idle you are stagnant; how then can anything be accomplished if one is stagnant? You get the point; nothing will be accomplished because your time is a key factor in all you do. Ecclesiastes 10:18 (KJV) says, "By much slothfulness the building decayeth; and through idleness of the hands the house droppeth through". In this verse, we can see the effect idleness can have when we mismanage our time. It cripples our ability to produce and achieve that which we were sent out to do. However, this is why honoring time is a major factor and aspect in maximizing a life of greatness. Another key component in honoring your time is being around other like-minded and disciplined people who seek the same interest and values time. Who you surround yourself with is important and if there is a healthy relationship, there will be healthy time management as well as the right boundaries that grant that time, we give ourselves to. The measure of time we give to others, things, and obligations should be based on our purpose, trust, and the will of God. One of the most abused areas of time is being late for events or starting behind time for an event as well as running late for work. Last year (2021) I was convicted greatly by the Holy Spirit because I was very slothful with my time on my job, and it affected my progress on my job and inconvenienced many others. My manager had to write me up and it was at this moment I realized I had an issue with honoring time in this area of my life. It didn't take long for me to get it together however, because I understood that if I was dishonorable with my time on my job it would spill over into other areas of my life that would be detrimental to my future and success in the years to come. See, sometimes we never take into consideration the effect our time management can have on others. My slothfulness and lateness to work caused my colleagues to work overtime and miss vital things in their personal life. It even caused frustration and strife on the job because they thought I was being inconsiderate. I didn't even know it until I was convicted by the Lord and received a write-up for my behavior. We must realize our failures before it is too late because if we don't, we will waste great and valuable time, that once again we can never get back. I knew better, but my knowing meant nothing if I wasn't willing to put my words and thoughts into action. We must not only talk a good game, but we must diligently practice what we preach. I encourage you that in all you get ready to step out to do honor your time, for it will profit you much and it will benefit many around you.

> So teach us to number our days, That we may cultivate and bring to You a heart of wisdom. **Psalms 90:12 AMP**

PRAYER

Today, we pray for a greater discipline over our time management and father we ask that you restore the time that was lost due to our inability to know and value our time. We pray that you will forgive us of our slothfulness as well as idleness and give us a second chance to make things right in every area of our lives. Dear Lord, we declare our time and our lives are in your hands and that from this day forward we will honor the time that has been granted unto us. In Jesus' precious name. Amen.

DAY 15

"True Friendship is Honorable"

One who has unreliable friends soon comes to ruin,
but there is a friend who sticks closer than a brother

PROVERBS 18:24 NIV

There is nothing more honoring in the world than to see two people who walk together on one accord in agreement and who honor one another.

A true friend, one that is there closer than a brother, a friend who is loyal, trustworthy, and a person who has no contempt in their hearts but love and honor genuinely. Yes, a true friendship is honorable; it brings support and stability. If we ever needed a code to crack open concerning honor, it would be friendship. Something rare and hard to come across and very difficult to keep, we desperately need true friends in this day and time. In fact, it is honorable according to the Word of God and at times, trumpets over one's relationship with his or her sibling. The Bible states a friend sticks closer than a brother which means a friend is highly valued and honored. A friend is a reliable source and is very vital to your growth and success. Friends hold you accountable and teach you things about yourself you never knew. Therefore, this is why we should never take any God-ordained friendship for granted as well as make sure you never miss the opportunity to appreciate that friend God has released into your life. The reason many don't have a friend or become alone is because they have either dishonored previous relationships or have yet to learn the key value, a true friendship has to offer. For unto the faithful or perhaps the honorable, they see friendship as an asset and as an advantage over their adversary, but a fool disregard knowledge and gratitude, from a sensible person. Friends come into our lives to sharpen us, and iron indeed sharpens iron (Proverbs 27:17). They love despite our circumstances and adversities and are always willing to lend a hand. A life without a friend is a life of misery and defeat. That is why the Bible teaches us that two are better than one. With friends, we can accomplish more and show the world what it means to be united. Take this scripture for example:

> Two are better than one, because they have a good return for their labor: If either of them falls down, one can help the other up. But pity anyone who falls and has no one to help them up. **(Ecclesiastes 4:9-10 NIV)**

In this Scripture, it is clear why we need friends but not only friends, but it also shows the importance of unity. Without the help of others, we are destined to fall, but with a spirit of humility and the support of others, we can conquer and succeed no matter what life may throw our way. The honor of a friend makes one's name great and establishes his or her repetition among noble men. The honor you show a friend is the honor others will give unto you. A man who plans on having friends must likewise show himself friendly. I find it very difficult to expect people to treat you a certain way if you haven't treated others with the same respect and honor. I remember when I was a kid my mom would say treat others how you want to be treated. In other words, what you sow you will reap. We can't expect to treat people badly and not expect the same fate. However, we must understand the principle of respect and honor while entering in and out of relationships because when we do so they are long-lasting and beneficial. When growing up I have always had the privilege to have friends around me, some closer than others, but I've always had a friend in my corner. One of the things I have learned throughout the years is that God will send a friend at your darkest hour. Yes, it is at those moments you are down and out or ready to give up; he will send the right friend along the way to encourage you and support you, so that you may continue to press forward with picking your head up knowing this is not the end. Some friends are sent with divine assignments, and this is why we should never compare our previous friendships to our present ones as well as compare those who are in your inner circle to those who may be at a greater distance in your life. Every friend is given its purpose, and it is best we learn the roles we each play in one another's life. Many times, we see confusion or a breach in our friendships because we misplace someone or forget the role they play within our life. When this happens, this can be very dangerous and can lead to separations rather than an unbreakable and strong covenant relationship. While I have learned quite a bit over the years, I have also made mistakes. The biggest mistake you can make is not keeping your word in your friendship and telling another's deepest secret. Within the lines of friendship, secrets are shared, and one must be trusted on holding those things confidential. This is in the same manner in which God wants to communicate with us, as a friend just as it was in the days of Abraham (James 2:23). When you have a true friend, you share secrets, and the friend who keeps those secrets are considered honorable and trustworthy. That is the reason I would charge you to stay trustworthy, honest, and loyal in any friendship that is worth having. It was friendships like David and Jonathan we can also learn a lot from. They had a friendship like no other. It was the most intimate relationship ever and was sealed before God. The Bible states that Jonathan made a covenant with David because he loved him as his own soul (1 Samuel 18:3). So much so, Jonathan turned on his own father to rescue and save David from the jealousy of his father, Saul, in true pursuit of their relationship and loyalty. Therefore, this is another reason why friendship is so honorable because it requires sincere sacrifice. Throughout David and Jonathan's relationship, we see a consistent sacrifice and reciprocity like none other. When there is a true friendship set in place it will require testing, to prove that friendship. I remember when I was in high school there was a bully on my football team picking on my best friend. So much so, that my best friend was about to quit the team because he couldn't take the bullying, and everyone in the locker room always laughing at him. However, they didn't do it to me as much because I was perhaps valuable and good (of good skill) on the team, but in my best friend's case it was his first year playing high school football and he was not used to how things went down in the locker room. Well on game day of one of those Fridays during 2nd period, we were in weightlifting class and this bully started picking on my best friend, but this time it wasn't funny and turned out to be roughly serious. My best friend got tired that day, a day we were supposed to be resting and preparing for a game that night, I find myself between my friend and this bully. It turns out that he wanted to push my best friend around and expected for him to continue to take the mistreatment, but however, I came in like a David that day standing up to Goliath. The thing was my best friend had not intended to fight my teammate, but once he told the bully to stop doing what he was doing to him, the bully got mad and wanted to pick a fight. I tried to calm things down, but instead, I found myself throwing fists punches and now at odds with my teammate. Once again, a Friday on game day when we were supposed to be resting. Yes, we were in a heavyweight boxing ring and this fight became the talk of the school. I'll never forget that day when I was called to step in and defend my friend who was wrongly being attacked. It was a day not only did our friendship bring honor to one another, but it also rendered justice. Although we got into a little trouble from our head coach, my friend never had to worry about that bully again because justice was served, and our friendship was proven in a greater capacity. Was it okay to fight? Of course not, but when you honor your friendships, no matter what the cause may be, always be willing to support, lend a hand, and make the proper sacrifice no matter the cost. My friend and I, our relationship was likened to that of David and Jonathan that day. Loyalty was at the fore front, and we vowed to always be there for one another. Yet, sometimes when we make these vows unto our friends, we never know the exact cost it will cost us, but we make these covenant agreements from a place of love and out of faith, knowing our faith will carry us through. A true friend is willing to walk with you, do life with you, and is always there to cover your back because true friendship will always bring honor.

> Though one may be overpowered, two can defend themselves. A cord of three strands is not quickly broken. **Ecclesiastes 4:12 NIV**

PRAYER

Dear heavenly Father, I pray that you will give us the right friends in this season. I pray that you will allow us to build long-lasting friendships that will impact the world and the lives around us. I declare we are coming into a greater capacity of love and unity in this hour and that every confusion spirit attached to our relationships would be dismantled and bonded in Jesus' mighty name. Give us relationships that will make our purpose come alive and friends who will stick no matter what life brings. This is my prayer in Jesus' precious name, Amen.

DAY 16

"Youths Require Honor"

Let no one look down on [you because of] your youth, but be an example and set a pattern for the believers in speech, in conduct, in love, in faith, and in [moral] purity.

1st TIMOTHY 4:12 AMP

One of the greatest groups of people who deserve and need honor in today's sociality are the youths. I believe we have dropped the ball on this generation in more ways than we know, and honor is one of the major issues. As a youth myself, there is hardly any honor given. For some reason, we live in a world where adults and elderly people have forgotten what it means to build or raise a generation on morals and values and likewise exemplify those same characteristics which also they, themselves have learned over the years. We desperately need men and women to arise unto the occasion and empower a dying generation of young people with the grace and capacity of honor. The lack of honor spills over into the next generation when it's not given or shown. Not only do our youths in this hour require honor but they deserve the honor. No one is exempt from the grace of honor, no matter their status or age. Throughout Scripture, we read that God would use and raise young men to do great exploits. Men such as Jeremiah, David, Joseph, and even King Josiah. God is not impressed with a person's age but rather their ability to yield themselves unto him and be obedient to all he says and commands, such as these are worthy of honor and deserve honor without any restraints. One of the most dangerous things one can ever do is measure someone by their age and fail to honor them. True honor sees no age but always finds its way to shine in the lives of others. I can recall a time in my life when I was denied honor because of my age and because of that moment before being delivered, it made me have a different outlook on life and those around me. Often, this will occur when you're only a teenager or while you're still learning and inexperienced towards different things and people who know better will find ways to take advantage of your youth. In this part of this 21-day pathway, it is my job to encourage and prepare you as a young man to another to not allow others to take advantage of you or walk over you because you are deserving of honor and should never struggle nor fight to have it given or shown. It was early in my ministry of 2014 when I was attending this church as a young minister not even licensed or doing a lot of preaching, I experienced the stench of dishonor from someone much older than myself. I remember them despising my youth because they had been in ministry for longer than I had and was saying things behind my back and sometimes to my face, all because my pastor was allowing me to have a key to the church and allowed me to preach here and there. They would often say things like "who does he think he is" I have kids his age or he doesn't know enough. These are the things that I would hear in this ministry because I was a young man zealous for the things of God. It wasn't easy going to Bible study every Thursday and going to church every Sunday because my spirit would be grieved on how people looked at me and thought such things about me when I was only trying to do the work of the lord. Their jealousy was getting the best of me until my pastor one day pulled me to the side and said the words "let no one despise your youth but be an example". Upon hearing those words from a man who believed in me and who also honored me, something that day rose in me to keep pressing and being that example no matter my age because I understood God wasn't concerned about age, but he was more concerned on how we love, obey and treat others. Though I wanted to give up, I found it within my spirit to keep going and being that example because I knew it was only the enemy who was trying to stop me and muzzle me. As young people, there will be times you are going to want to quit but I challenge you to keep going and as elders, I challenge you to keep pushing and honor the youth. If it wasn't for my pastor that day I don't know where I would be in my life right now. In addition, it is important the young and old run together. I am persuaded that there is a merging of generations coming together in this hour who will show the world what true honor looks like when young people and the elderly come together willingly and unselfishly. We see this in the book of Proverbs, the key importance's of both young and old: "The glory of young men is their [physical] strength, And the honor of aged men is their gray head [representing wisdom and experience]" (Proverbs 20:29AMP). When we see these facets and elements of both coming together, we get a dual anointing of wisdom and strength that can't be denied nor reckoned because the humility of both young and old find a way to partner and unite for the greater good. Once more this is a key component in this hour and an area the Lord is truly highlighting because of the lack of honor that has gone forth over the last few decades. The solution is honor being restored as fathers and mothers take a stand to show the youth what it means and what it looks like to carry and give honor. Young people are precious in the eyes of God, and he expects that elders would groom them and nourish them for his service (Ephesians 6:4) so that they would be successful in all walks of life. We are living in a crucial time, and we need not argue or bicker, but we need a merging of generations to stand together and flourish. This is what the book of Malachi was talking about when he prophesied, "See, I will send the prophet Elijah to you before that great and dreadful day of the Lord comes. He will turn the hearts of the parents to their children, and the hearts of the children to their parents; or else I will come and strike the land with destruction (Malachi 4:5-6). He was implementing and referencing a dynasty and an unbridle generation, coming together and restoring as well as aligning old and young once again and I believe we will see it in this day and time as honor goes forth, especially with the youth. Youths require and deserve honor, let's be a people to give it and display it unselfishly.

> And the child grew, and waxed strong in spirit, filled with wisdom: and the grace of God was upon him. **LUKE 2:40 KJV**

PRAYER

Father, I declare in this hour we will see youths rising to do great things for the kingdom of God. Father, we ask that you raise up honorable young men who will lead by example. I pray that they will walk like Jesus in love, faith, and purity. Lord, we thank you for giving us young people on earth who are strong and intelligent, and we declare you bless their youths all the days of their lives. In Jesus' mighty name we pray, Amen.

DAY 17

"Great Honor is Shown Within Love"

Be devoted to one another in love.
Honor one another above yourselves.

ROMANS 12:10NIV

Has it ever occurred unto you that the reason for the poor response we get from others is because of our inability to love? Yes, in fact, the reason we don't see as much honor or respect may be that we have failed to love others. It has been proven over and over throughout time that great honor is shown within love. Love is the center of it all and should always be our primary reason for whatever we do. It's through that place of love we can see genuine honor and not the one you force to give or must feel pressured but loving from a pure place, produces the mind and heart of honor. We are not subject to only love once but the Bible is clear that we should be devoted to love. That means wearing it upon us as if it was the very clothing on our bodies. The purpose of love and honor is that it is meant to be given unto others above ourselves, so if we don't give it out then what's the purpose of carrying it? If we don't have the heart or the stomach to love, then how can honor truly exist? Everything is built on the soul-tie of love and honor and without the two the foundation lay in ruins. It is sad to say, but we live in a heartless world. Not only do we seek honor, but we also have to restore love because it waxes cold. Behind every problem, there is a root cause and today, we are empty of love. I believe we are living in perilous times; a time when men would be lovers of themselves, and a time honor will be lacking (2 Timothy 2:15). However, there is still a remnant of people in the world that refuse to see the nations and communities die unto the rebellion of those who will purposely refuse and deny showing love and honor. The time is now that we will witness a people who will reject what is not of God and cling on to that which is pure and holy. Loving others and God are not an option or a matter of negotiation, but it is the very DNA and cup one should eagerly drink from. I often tell people that if you have a hard time down here on earth loving and honoring then you're going to have a hard time in heaven when we are all summoned together for all eternity. When Jesus comes back, he is looking for your love. Not how much money you have, how big your house or church is, or rather how well you've served but he is looking for a love walk. Many times, we are focused on how successful we are in other areas, but the question is how successful our love is for others? The true maximize life of success is measured and marked by one's love for others. Your capacity to love will either advance you or hinder you. You can always tell the level of honor someone carries by their talk of love and gratitude for others. Love anchors the character of real leaders and they understand that without love their ship is soon to sink if love is not steering them. That is why it is our duty and obligation to love and when we do, honor spills out. For centuries many have tried to separate the two (love & honor) but I believe they are much alike. Where love shows great affection and honor is to think about something in high regard. No doubt, both abilities give us the grace to share with others and hold them in great regard. If you love something you hold it in high regard but if you fail to love something, you risk the mistake of dishonoring it, and this is why love and honor need no separation. When we love, our honor is shown, blessings are unfolded and most importantly wisdom will be released. One of the greatest gifts God could have ever given us is the ability to love and we should never place our love in the wrong hands or take it for granted. Where there is great hate and betrayal, love should be our weapon of defense. The Bible says, *"Love is patient, love is kind. It does not envy, it does not boast, it is not proud. It does not dishonor others, it is not self-seeking, it is not easily angered, it keeps no record of wrongs" (1 Corinthians 13:4-5).* Our love defensive arsenal can fight against things that try to hold us down or in bondage because it is always seeking the heart and will of God; love is God, and it needs no other illustration or example. As we set upon a new pathway of honor, I believe love is another key element that will get the wheel turning and moving if we would only open our hearts once again to love. Without love, we can do nothing, and it is time we realize our kingdom authority when we partner and reflect love in the earth. Did you know that to love is to obey? According to John 14:15, Jesus gives us a command that if we love him keep and obey his commandments. The action we take to love someone is the humility we use to obey the father. The Bible also speaks of the hypocrisy many of us make when we say we love God but hate our brother. How can we say we love someone we have never seen and hate our brother whom we've seen? The person who does this is not of God and does not understand the eternal love of God. Never forget we love because he first loved us, by giving His one only begotten Son to die for all humanity. If you're going to go deeper in honoring, you must be willing to go deeper in your love walk. Those who love, know that the father abides in them. Therefore, for this reason, the last two years have been a bit tough because of the pandemic and I believe the world at large has been on a love walk, where God has been healing and restoring broken relationships. During the pandemic, we have been forced to stay in our homes with our family, those we didn't once fellowship with and some we hadn't seen in years or because of busy life affairs but because of the lockdowns and mandates it has caused a great restoration in households and it has caused many to appreciate each other the more because of the many death tolls we have experienced throughout the 2 years. I do not believe this was some sort of coincidence, but I believe God used this moment to get the attention of many, to restore love and honor. If you're going to be effective on your love walk it must first start at home and one of the major things God wants to do in this hour is restore families and build them back on the premise of Honor and love. Honor starts at home and if you can't do it at home, you will stand a poor chance of doing it anywhere else. As you have been challenged on this day to love my prayer is that it will bring out a greater honor within you and from today you will always love and place others above yourself to represent the kingdom of God. For indeed this is what true and great love models.

> And this commandment we have from Him, that the one who loves God should also [unselfishly] love his brother *and* seek the best for him.
> **1 John 4:21 AMP**

PRAYER

Heavenly Father, today, our prayer is that you will touch the hearts of your people and that you will heal the brokenhearted. Lord, we ask that you bring relationships to a place of wholeness and allow love to be shown in a greater capacity unto the world. May we always remain tendered hearted towards your people reflecting honor and humility and anchoring ourselves even more in the clouds of love. May love always be our guide and be the premise of all we do in Jesus' precious name, Amen.

DAY 18

"Honor is a Sword of Justice"

Mighty king, glorious ruler, strap on your sword and ride out in splendor!
Win victories for truth and mercy and justice.
Do fearsome things with your powerful arm

PSALMS 45:3-4 CEV

You have heard it said time after time that honor is a code of justice. Make no mistake about it, honor is a sword that swings when it comes down to justice. In this day and time, we eagerly need those who will rise to carry the sword of honor that will liberate and bring justice unto their communities and nations. I believe we are in a critical era where many have refuted justice and become comfortable with injustice because of impure motives and the compromising of money and greed. Rather it is in the church, in business, or our government we have no honor for justice. However, I'm convinced and persuaded that we will begin to see the emergence of justice being enthroned once again on the earth. Justice is something, we all can use in our everyday life. Justice can be defined as: "just behavior or treatment" according to Webster dictionary. I also like to define justice as the ability to walk in integrity or righteousness. More than ever, we need righteousness and a people who will walk integral before the Lord.

It means to have morals and values for the things that are right and refraining from the things which are evil and wrong. When walking upright before the father, it is the code of honor we open because we are exemplifying the God we serve that is just. *"He is the Rock, his works are perfect, and all his ways are just. A faithful God who does no wrong, upright and just is he" (Deuteronomy 32:4NIV).*

Throughout history we can find many men & women who reformed and pioneered justice and that later brought honor unto their name. It was noble people like Queen Esther in her day who brought a sword of justice when she stopped the king bravely from killing innocent Jews (Esther 8:4-5). We also find those such as Rosa Parks, Dr. Martin Luther King Jr, Nelson Mandela, and many others who model justice and honor during their day and time to change the world forever. These men and women risked everything to serve in a time of uncertainty to make the world a better place and to exemplify justice, proving that the world is a better place when justice is delegated. They were up against all odds, but they knew that bringing justice was the honorable thing to do. Today they are recognized as noble and honorable civil right leaders and has marked this generation beyond measures. See, it doesn't take a lot to bring justice, but what it takes is courage and faith to do something that has never been done before andit's at that moment true honor is manifested. The Bible speaks of the sword of truth which also represents justice; God has given unto all of us that sword, so that we may rightly divide what is right and what is wrong. This sword is intended to expose the corrupt and the wickedness that lies within the world but also to shine light on those things which are hidden to bring freedom and vindication for those who have suffered and for those who've been oppressed. When justice is properly rendered there is a joy that comes over entire nations and peace begins to wrap that nation causing unity, love, and even prosperity. This is why the Bible states that when the righteous rule the people rejoice (Proverbs 29:2). When people witness justice and see that it is served fairly, there is undeniable happiness that is poured out upon them, and that gives them hope. One day while preparing to write this book I found myself sitting in my living room and while sitting I noticed my kids watching this movie about this little mouse who was a hero and who helped establish justice throughout his village and earned a badge of honor because he was willing to go the extra mile. In that moment the Lord began to give me a divine revelation. Although this was a cartoon movie, the Lord was trying to get a message across to me. I realize that if you're going to have a badge of honor, you must not look at how small you are and you must be willing to go the extra mile to bring forth justice regardless of what may try to come your way. As I continued to watch the movie, I then understood that big things come in little packages. Here it is God was using this little mouse to teach me a valuable lesson, that I'll later be sharing today but this mouse in this movie had the code of honor. I often watch movies that relate to knights and kings and each time, I see the importance of honor and justice and how the two complimented one another. Within the lines of these movies, knights and kings would be given a sword symbolic of their service and as a gift of honor. In movies such as these, we can learn a lot because they reflect the heart and will of God and teach us how vital justice is and shows the magnitude in which honor is supposed to be displayed. In essence, to honor, being a sword of justice, I believe we need to grab hold of it because in doing so we will see the hand of God move and we will see the liberation of many in more ways than we can imagine. When we partner with justice it becomes the anchor of others' hope. As we have come to the end of this day, I encourage you to walk upright and always be willing to render justice unto those around you, for injustice cannot stand against you because you've been given a sword of justice that establishes honor among the multitude.

When justice is done, it brings joy to the righteous but terror to evildoers.
Proverbs 21:15 NIV

PRAYER

Dear Holy Spirit, we pray that you teach us your ways that we may render justice in the earth and that we may bring glory and honor unto your name. We declare that justice will reign throughout the nations and peace would be released like never before. Make us righteous and give us the boldness to always stand for justice in Jesus' mighty name, Amen.

DAY 19

"Honor the Process"

I have seen something else under the sun: The race is not to the swift or the battle to the strong, nor does food come to the wise or wealth to the brilliant or favor to the learned; but time and chance happen to them all.

ECCLESIASTES 9:11 NIV

Since I've taken the time out to write this book, I have learned the importance of time and the process of creating something great and worthwhile. When I started this book a few months ago I thought I'll be done in a few weeks, but I was wrong because I have now been writing this book for 7 months. I was so zealous to get the book done that I was about to miss the lesson God was showing me through the book and it's honoring the process. Before greatness can be birthed there must be a process that something or someone goes through. Mines so happen to be with this book. We live in a time where many rushes or that are impatient, but I believe that there is a lot we can learn from the process. It's in the process we learn skills, our character is refined, and we experience a wealth of knowledge and gain an abundance of wisdom. The process isn't meant to hurt you but build you and grow you. I've seen many over the years who have abandoned the process for quick success and failed to keep the success because they didn't have the endurance to stand when tough times came knocking at their door. If we abandon the process, we risk the chances of making major mistakes and getting ourselves hurt. When we honor the process, we inherit a grace of excellence and surpass years of pain and sorrow. Those who obtain great success understand the importance of being still and the language of the process. The process teaches us valuable lessons and also helps us to develop a stronger relationship with God. I can recall the story of the children of Israel while being in the wilderness, in the book of Numbers and how they had to depend on God for everything and had to trust that he would provide. Often God would use these moments to see if we would totally depend on him and to teach us how to wait in the process. It is not God's heart that we rush nor be anxious for anything. This is also why the Bible commands that we should pray and give thanks, refraining and relinquishing from all forms of hastiness or anxiousness (Philippians 4:6-7). When we honor the process, we later appreciate it and gain stamina within our minds and body as well as within our heart and we become mentally stable. In the place of the wilderness or the process,there are some encounters we have with God we wouldn't have had if we didn't go through the process; so, while you're in your process I encourage you to honor it and enjoy it. Many times, while in the place of the process we tend to overlook the small beginnings because we are so focused on getting to the finish line but it's in those small stages of our process, we gain key and vital wisdom. Like the saying goes "good things come unto those who wait". The problem is we are living in a society that doesn't know how to wait because everyone wants a quick fix or a quick come up. Remember, that the Bible teaches that "*...those who wait on the Lord Shall renew their strength; They shall mount up with wings like eagles, They shall run and not be weary, They shall walk and not faint" (Isaiah 40:31NKJV)*

Nevertheless, it's through the place of process our strength is renewed and it's only afterward we are ready and can soar, going places we have never been. What God is looking for in this season is people who will honor the process and who will allow him to refine them as well as heal them. As you have read each day leading up to this day be empowered and encouraged knowing that God is not looking for you to be perfect, but he is looking for a person who will take him by the hand so that he can lead them through the process. There may be dilemmas in life, but the one who honors the process will succeed. Remember the father will never, put too much on you that you can't bear! The process will fortify your destiny.

> I am convinced *and* confident of this very thing, that He who has begun a good work in you will [continue to] perfect *and* complete it until the day of Christ Jesus [the time of His return] **Philippians 1:6 AMP**

PRAYER

Today, we ask that you help us navigate the process and that you give us the endurance and strength to keep going. Help us to never dishonor our small beginnings or to get ahead of you. Father, continue to position us for greatness and give us the courage to subdue all odds in Jesus' mighty name, Amen.

DAY 20

"HONOR LESSONS: HOMEWORK"

Wisdom is the principal thing; therefore, get wisdom: and with all thy getting get understanding.

PROVERBS 4:7

Today, I challenge you to look deep within to see where you need help and guidance concerning honor. As you have read this book, I want you to reflect on the areas that have truly been impactful and the ones that have challenged you in more ways than others. Examine yourself today and list 5 areas you still need equipping and write out the solutions and goals you plan on taking to achieve those goals. Remember: to maximize your honor for greatness, you must be willing to take the steps and apply the wisdom set before you. I challenge you once more, to crack open the code of honor. You were built for this!

ASSESSMENT

- What was your favorite day and what did you learn?
- What day challenged you the most?

- What does honor mean to you since reading this book?
- What areas can you grow more in concerning honor?
- What advice can you offer others concerning honor and what steps will you take when you don't see honor being displayed?

DAY 21

"The Honor Code: access granted"

Open up, ancient gates! Open up, ancient doors, and let the King of glory enter.

PSALMS 24:9 NLT

Wow, I am excited about your future! You have now entered a new level and dimension of honor since coming alongside with me throughout this 21-day pathway. It is my pleasure and honor to reassure you that your best days are ahead of you and that there is nothing that can stop you or stand in your way because you now know and understand the different facets of honor and what it means. Your days of striving and great endeavors await you. As we have come to the end of this book, I pray you were blessed, restored, and revived. For God has a plan for your life and it will take pure honor to fulfill it. Always remember that honor starts within the mind and flows from without the heart. When honor is in the atmosphere, the King of glory can enter. It is the honor of God that we as a people show and display honor in the earth. The honor code was established to help you maximize your honor for greatness and I truly believe that as you have been a student of God's word and have postured

\\yourself to follow these examples you will be that honorable nobleman, that many can only dream of. Never give up, go the extra mile, and watch as the code of honor manifests. Welcome to your season of granted access because you have learned to steward honor well.

FINAL PRAYER

Lord, we thank you and honor you! We worship and adore you for you are great and mighty and no one is like you. We thank you for allowing us to make it through this entire 21-day pathway and we thank you in advance for causing people to honor and favor us. May we grow in wisdom and stature and may the honor code of access always be forever granted unto us all in Jesus' precious and holy name, Amen.

REFERENCES

Bible Gateway.https://Biblegateway.com.

Merriam-Webster.com Dictionary, Merriam Webster. https://www.merriam-webster.com/dictionary.

BOOK RECOMMENDATIONS

The Prophetic Manual: Cultivating a Prophetic Community

By: Dontrell J. Green Sr.

Mastering Your Warfare

By: Madeline James

I Will NOT

By: Bishop Greg D. Gill

Winds of His Spirit

By: Daniel Emerson

Made in the USA
Las Vegas, NV
13 February 2025

17969301R00059